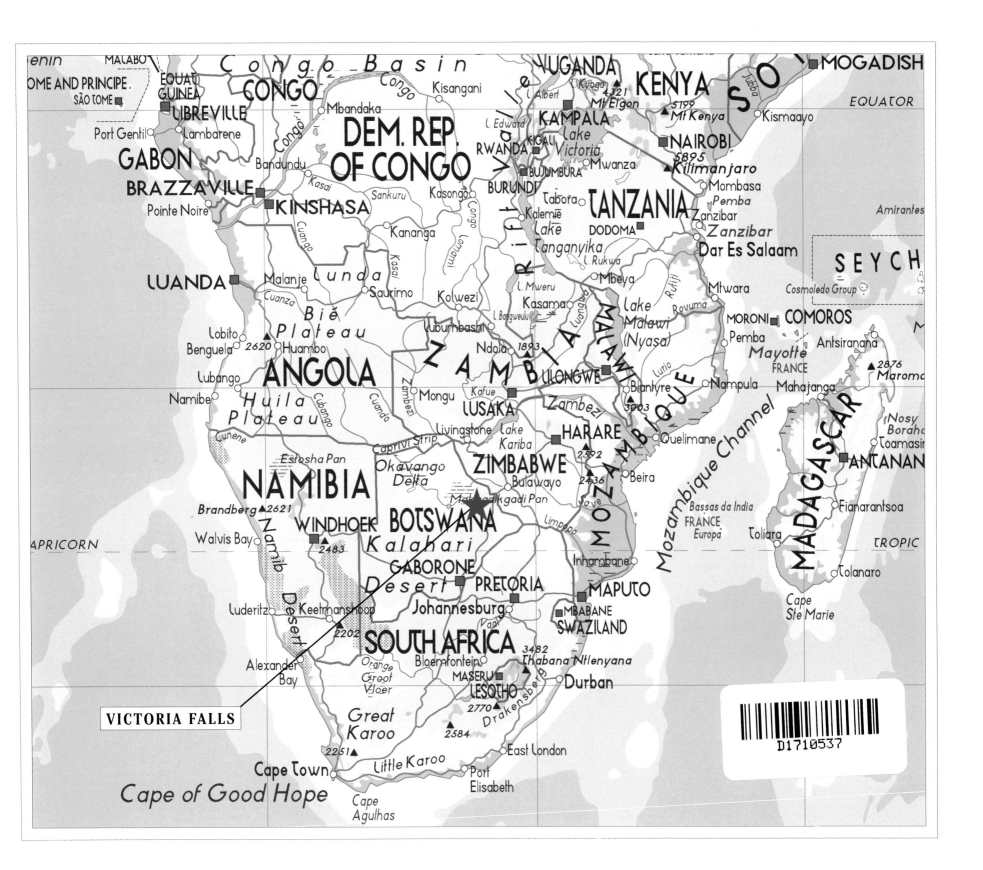

Published by Creative Education
123 South Broad Street
Mankato, Minnesota 56001

Creative Education is an imprint of The Creative Company.

Designed by Stephanie Blumenthal
Production design by The Design Lab

Photographs by Corbis (Albright-Knox Art Gallery, Anthony Bannister; Gallo Images, Bettmann, Richard Bickel, Nigel J. Dennis; Gallo Images, Aron Frankental; Gallo Images, GIRAUD PHILIPPE/CORBIS SYGMA, Roger De La Harpe; Gallo Images, Historical Picture Archive, Eric and David Hosking, Colin Hoskins; Cordaiy Photo Library Ltd., Hulton-Deutsch Collection, Japack Company, Peter Johnson, Charles & Josette Lenars, Craig Lovell, Ludovic Maisant, Buddy Mays, Richard T. Nowitz, David Reed, Galen Rowell, Royalty-Free, Rykoff Collection, Paul A. Souders, Swim Ink, Underwood & Underwood, Patrick Ward, Nik Wheeler), Geoatlas/World Vector 3 Map CD

Printed in the United States of America

Library of Congress Cataloging-in-Publication Data

Kalz, Jill.
Victoria Falls / by Jill Kalz.
p. cm. — (Natural wonders of the world)
Summary: Describes the world's largest waterfall, located in southern
Africa, discussing its geology, exploration, and conservation.
ISBN 1-58341-327-8
1. Victoria Falls (Zambia and Zimbabwe)—Description and travel—Juvenile literature.
[1. Victoria Falls (Zambia and Zimbabwe)] I. Title. II. Series.

DT3140.V54K38 2004   916.891—dc22   2003065230

First edition

2 4 6 8 9 7 5 3 1

VICTORIA FALLS

JILL KALZ

CREATIVE EDUCATION

THE TRAVELING WATERFALL

Victoria Falls is not the highest waterfall in the world. That honor belongs to Angel Falls, in southeastern Venezuela, South America, whose water plummets 3,212 feet (979 m)—a drop nearly 10 times higher than that of Victoria Falls.

Victoria Falls reigns as the world's largest wall of water, plummeting into a deep gash on the Zimbabwe/Zambia border in Africa.

It is made of water, yet it smokes. It roars like rolling thunder under clear, blue skies. Although it is one of Earth's greatest natural wonders, it remained hidden from the world outside Africa until just 150 years ago. It mesmerizes, terrifies, and humbles—all at once. Dropping hundreds of feet into a deep gash in the earth's surface, bewitching all who see and hear it, Victoria Falls is a waterfall like no other.

Victoria Falls is the largest falling curtain of water in the world. Located in southern Africa, on the border between Zambia and Zimbabwe, the Falls measure nearly one mile (1.6 km) wide—one and a half times the width of North America's Niagara Falls. Fed by the Zambezi River, the Falls drop more than 350 feet (105 m), sending white, smoke-like clouds of spray high into the air. On average, 130 million gallons (490 million l) of water spill over the **lip** of the Falls every minute. That's enough to fill more than 100 Olympic-size swimming pools! The falling water rumbles so loudly that it can often be heard as far away as 20 miles (32 km).

Geologists attribute the formation of Victoria Falls to the **erosive** power of moving water. About 150 million years ago, molten lava from deep inside the earth rose through the planet's surface and covered the landscape of ancient Africa. Once the lava cooled, it turned into basalt rock. As the rock hardened, it **contracted,**

About 100 miles (160 km) downstream from Victoria Falls lies Lake Kariba, one of the world's largest artificial lakes. Created by the construction of a 40-story-high dam across the Zambezi River, Lake Kariba measures 20 miles (32 km) wide and 170 miles (275 km) long.

The quiet, slow-moving waters of the upper Zambezi River give little warning of the imposing waterfall ahead.

creating a network of fissures, or cracks— major fissures running east and west, linked by smaller ones running north and south.

Millions of years passed, and rivers began to flow. Geologists believe that the upper portion of today's Zambezi was once a separate river that flowed down Zimbabwe's western border, along its southern border, and emptied into the Indian Ocean. About two million

years ago, however, parts of the earth's crust slowly rose, blocking the river's path to the sea. Water pooled behind the blockage and created a huge inland lake. Eventually, this water spilled onto the surrounding landscape, carved a new course for the river, and met up with the middle portion of today's

Zambezi. There, the upper river fell 820 feet (250 m) over an **escarpment**, creating the "original" Victoria Falls.

The fast-falling water then started to erode the lip of the Falls and cut a deep channel into the rock along a large east-west fissure, gradually moving the Falls upstream. At one point, the river valley turned north, and the water wore away at a small, north-south crack. That crack eventually linked with another large east-west fissure. As the water eroded the rock, a broad, curtain-like **cataract** formed. This process was repeated eight times, resulting in the eight zigzagging **gorges** visible today downstream from the Falls. Each gorge once held a magnificent waterfall.

6

Rainbows form when the sun's rays reflect off raindrops or mist. Because of the ever-present spray rising from the Falls, and the area's mostly sunny skies, rainbows are a common sight over the falling water. Sometimes, moonlight shining through the spray can cause "lunar rainbows," which are more white than multi-colored.

HOME ON THE ZAMBEZI

There are actually five separate waterfalls of varying widths that make up Victoria Falls. Small islands located near the lip of the Falls force the Zambezi to flow around them, dividing the river into the Devil's Cataract, Main Falls, Horseshoe Falls, Rainbow Falls, and Eastern Cataract.

The river responsible for Victoria Falls starts as a spring hundreds of miles away, in northwestern Zambia. The Zambezi is Africa's fourth longest river behind the Nile, the Zaire (Congo), and the Niger. A few miles upstream from the Falls, the wide, relatively shallow river moves along at a sluggish pace and is dotted by a series of islands. Some are no more than sandbars covered with reeds. Others support dense woodlands. There are no rapids to warn of the dangerous drop ahead, just a low, persistent rumble and clouds of spray rising in the distance.

A variety of grasses and moisture-loving trees such as palms, mopanes, and acacias line the upper Zambezi riverbanks. The hard fruits and blood-red flowers of the sausage tree hang down from its limbs on long, ropelike stalks. Resembling sticks of sausage, the fruits grow up to two feet (61 cm) long and may weigh 15 pounds (7 kg) or more. Once the tree's flowers drop to the ground, impalas, bush pigs, or small antelope called duikers may eat them.

The baobab is one of the most recognizable trees along the Zambezi, with its barrel-shaped trunk and spidery crown. Its trunk is designed to store water and may measure up

Baobabs are one of the most useful trees on the African plains, providing shelter for small animals and insects, and nesting sites for birds such as hornbills and red-billed buffalo-weavers. Local peoples use the bark fiber for rope and cloth, the leaves and seeds for food, and the roots for medicinal tonics.

Vegetation on the Zambezi riverbanks ranges from common grasses and flowering plants to the unusual baobabs (opposite) and sausage trees (bottom right).

Caterpillars of the *Gonimbrasia* moth, which feed on mopane tree leaves, are a key source of protein for many rural communities in western Zimbabwe. Known as "mopane worms," these long-haired caterpillars are roasted fresh, or dried and mixed with crushed chilies as a crispy side dish.

to 40 feet (12 m) around! One baobab near Victoria Falls is thought to be more than 1,000 years old.

Crocodiles and pods of hippos cool themselves in the upper river's clear, clean water—closely watched by herons nesting in nearby reeds. Fish such as tiger fish and bream are plentiful. Zebras, elephants, water buffalo, monkeys, giraffes, rhinos, and hundreds of bird and insect species call the area flanking the upper Zambezi home, as do various snakes and rodents. One of the smallest river dwellers, the mosquito, is actually one of the deadliest. Mosquitoes thrive in areas of still or slow-moving water and can carry **malaria**. At dusk, hungry bats fill the air to feast on them.

Once the Zambezi spills over the lip of the Falls, it thunders into the steep-walled, narrow

gorge below, creating great clouds of spray. This ever-present mist, along with average year-round temperatures of 68 °F (20 °C), helps to sustain an environment similar to a **rainforest** on the land opposite the Falls. Lush vegetation, including a variety of ferns, mosses, and grasses, carpets the landscape. Wild date palms and fig trees sway under the weight of their fruits. The branches of ebony trees, mahogany trees, and other tall hardwoods form dark-green canopies high in the air.

The "rainforest" also supports a variety of wildlife, including vervet monkeys, baboons, warthogs, and small striped antelope called bushbucks. Black eagles and Taita falcons are among the estimated 400 species of birds that live in the greater Victoria Falls region.

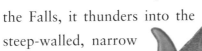

The lush plant life of the upper Zambezi supports a number of large herbivores, including elephants (top left), hippos (bottom left), and zebras (bottom right). It also feeds a variety of insects, such as the mopane caterpillar (opposite), which in turn are eaten by carnivores such as the black eagle (top right).

Animals of all shapes and sizes call the Victoria Falls region home. Second only to the elephant as the world's largest land mammal, the white rhinoceros (right) stands five to six feet (1.5–1.8 m) tall and weighs up to 6,000 pounds (2,700 kg). By contrast, the delicate bushbuck (below), stands less than three feet (90 cm) tall and weighs just 100 pounds (45 kg).

Special adaptations allow many different species to live closely together in the Falls region without having to compete for food. Giraffes (left) browse on foliage 7 to 16 feet (2–5 m) from the ground—too high for other herbivores to reach. The kingfisher (top) has a long, stout bill perfect for catching insects such as grasshoppers.

SMOKE THAT THUNDERS

Dr. Livingstone spent a total of 30 years in Africa, exploring nearly a third of the continent. Upon his death in 1873, his body was shipped to London, England, for burial. His heart, however, was buried in African soil, according to his final wishes.

Dr. David Livingstone (right) was so revered by the natives of the Falls region that a town was named in his honor.

Victoria Falls was one of southern Africa's greatest secrets until 1855, when a Scottish physician and **missionary** named Dr. David Livingstone, sailing the Zambezi River in search of the Indian Ocean, first set eyes on it. But Livingstone didn't discover the Falls. Since Victoria Falls had already existed for more than a million years, **indigenous** peoples called the Khoisan or "Bushmen" were the first to fall under the cataract's spell. The remains of their primitive tools, which date back to the Stone

Age, have been found in the sands around the Falls.

Around 1500, a group of migrants from northern Africa called the Tonga settled in the area. Skilled in pottery-making and agriculture, these peaceful people established small farming communities and inter-married with the Khoisan. The Tonga called the Falls *Shongwe*, meaning "a seething cauldron." Two islands at the lip of the Falls served as places of worship from which the Tonga sacrificed animals into the thundering water to please

1 6

The ancient art of pottery-making is still practiced today by Tonga women in the Victoria Falls region. Pots are made for cooking or storing water. Other crafts include the creation of objects used for healing or divination, such as this bird's nest pouch (opposite).

The Tonga believe that a serpent-like spirit named Nyaminyami inhabits the waters of the Zambezi. They say that when pleased, the river god provides fish and even offers strips of its own flesh as food. But when angered, it shakes the earth, causes devastating floods, and pulls canoeists into deadly whirlpools.

their rain god. In the early 1830s, the raiding Makololo people conquered the Tonga, and it was the Makololo who named the Falls *Mosi-oa-Tunya*—"the smoke that thunders."

Although some historians have suggested that various Portuguese or Arab explorers were the first outsiders to see the Falls, Livingstone is credited with bringing Victoria Falls to the attention of the world.

Livingstone christened the waterfall "Victoria Falls" in honor of Queen Victoria, who ruled Britain from 1837 to 1901, longer than any other British king or queen. The Scottish explorer logged the following description of his first encounter with the Falls in his journal in 1855: "After twenty minutes' sail [by canoe] from Kalai we came in sight...of the columns of vapor appropriately called 'smoke,' rising at a distance of five or six miles [8–10 km], exactly as when large tracts of grass are burned in Africa.... the tops of the columns at this distance appeared to mingle with the

In 1855, the beauty of Victoria Falls, named after Queen Victoria of England (opposite), inspired Livingstone to write, "One sees nothing but a dense white cloud. . . . From this cloud rushed up a great jet of vapor exactly like steam, and it mounted 200 or 300 feet [60- 90 m] high; there condensing, it changed its hue to that of dark smoke, and came back in a constant shower, which soon wetted us to the skin."

Commissioned by British financier Cecil Rhodes and completed in 1905, Victoria Falls railway bridge is an expanse of metal 200 feet (60 m) long that spans the gorge downstream from the Falls, connecting Zambia and Zimbabwe. Its completion signaled a turning point for the area, jump-starting the Victoria Falls tourism industry.

clouds. They were white below, and higher up became dark, so as to simulate smoke very closely. The whole scene was extremely beautiful. . . . scenes so lovely must have been gazed upon by angels in their flight."

After Dr. Livingstone's "discovery," and the discovery of coal and copper deposits in Zambia and Zimbabwe, white settlers began moving into the area, working as miners, hunters, traders, and missionaries. By 1903, a small European settlement called Old Drift, located about six miles (10 km) upstream from the Falls, in Zambia, boasted nearly 70 residents. Unfortunately, the village was built on low-lying, marshy land, which served as an ideal breeding ground for mosquitoes, and many residents died of malaria. The remaining settlers moved to higher ground and established Constitution Hill, where the town of Livingstone, an increasingly popular tourism hub, stands today.

20

During the early 1900s, scores of white settlers poured into the Victoria Falls region, including missionaries (top and bottom left), game hunters (bottom right), and diamond miners (top right). Their journeys into the area were made easier by the completion of the Victoria Falls railway bridge (opposite), which opened in 1905.

RUNNING ON ADRENALINE

The erosive power of the Zambezi's falling water shows no sign of weakening, as it's already eating away the rock along another fault line. Geologists predict that this line, located on the Falls' western end, will form a new perpendicular waterfall a few thousand years from now.

The Victoria Falls region offers tourists plenty of recreational opportunities, from high-energy bridge bungee jumping (right) to tranquil elephant safaris (opposite).

The mighty waterfall itself is the most popular attraction today in the Victoria Falls region. But a growing number of visitors are lured to the area by the tumultuous waters in the gorges downstream. Offering some of the most dangerous white-water rapids in the world, the lower Zambezi has prompted many to call the nearby town of Victoria Falls ("Vic Falls"), Zimbabwe, the "Adrenaline Capital of the World," attracting hordes of rafters and body boarders each year. Kayaking, canoeing, and fishing excursions are also popular activities, as are walking **safaris**, horseback trail rides, and hang gliding. Bungee jumpers flock to the middle of Victoria Falls bridge, which spans the Zambezi River downstream from the Falls, to experience a 365-foot

(111 m) fall. Less-adventurous types may ride an old-fashioned steam train across the bridge or sail the upper Zambezi on wildlife-watching boat cruises.

The Victoria Falls tourism industry kicked into high gear in the late 1980s. In 1991, an estimated 150,000 people visited the area. In 1995, that number doubled. During the late '90s, when tourism dollars flowed freely, the town of Vic Falls was highly **commercialized**, with new hotels, casinos, and tour companies springing up at a frantic pace. Analysts predicted that by 2006, more than one million tourists would descend upon the Falls each year.

However, Falls tourism declined dramatically at the turn of the 21st century. One reason was that Zimbabwe's poorly managed

Established in 1904, Zimbabwe's Victoria Falls Hotel (right), also called the "Grand Old Lady of the Falls," has offered guests breathtaking views of Victoria Falls for more than 100 years. During that time, the Edwardian-styled hotel has hosted some of the world's most rich and famous, including royalty, film stars, sports heroes, and politicians.

political system discouraged many travelers from visiting over concerns for their safety. Accusations of ballot tampering during the 2000 election and the violent takeover of hundreds of white-owned commercial farms throughout the country prompted would-be Falls tourists to visit nearby Zambia instead. In fact, many of the top hotel managers, chefs, and tour guides from Vic Falls crossed the river to Livingstone, injecting new life into that town.

Conservationists aren't sorry to see the tourism numbers drop. More tourists, they claim, mean more trash and human waste, which could pollute the river if not disposed of properly. As the number of people participating in water activities increases, the chances of them disturbing nesting sites for aquatic birds increase as well. And with large numbers of adventurers climbing in and out of the gorges, erosion becomes a threat, wearing away the nutrients needed by the area's vegetation and destroying vital animal habitats.

But no matter what governments say or do, how much money changes hands, or which towns thrive or fold, Victoria Falls will continue to spill over its hard lip and, at its own slow pace, carve its way farther upstream. Its soaking spray and the thunder of its pounding water will continue to fill the African sky as it has for thousands of years, and coat the skin of those who are willing to stop, listen, and feel all it has to say.

VICTORIA  FALLS

SEEING THE WONDER

The natural beauty of Victoria Falls and the Zambezi River draws thousands of camera-toting tourists each year from all over the world. Falls visitors are encouraged to pack plenty of film, as it is difficult to obtain locally, especially in Zambia.

Because Victoria Falls lies on the border between two countries, visitors have the option of traveling to its south side (Zimbabwe) or its north side (Zambia)—or both! The easiest way to get to Victoria Falls is to fly into Johannesburg, South Africa, and then connect by smaller plane to Livingstone (Zambia) or Vic Falls (Zimbabwe). Accommodations, restaurants, and gift shops are plentiful in either town, and both are small enough to explore on foot. Livingstone has a more relaxed, true African feel to it, while Vic Falls is heavily commercialized.

The best time to visit is in the dry, winter months of May through August, when daytime temperatures average a comfortable 79 °F (26 °C). Winter skies are usually clear and sunny, so be sure to pack sunscreen, sunglasses, and a hat. Avoid wearing brightly colored or white clothes if you're planning to go on a wildlife-watching safari, as the animals will see you more easily, making it difficult for you to get close. Choose neutral colors such as khaki instead. Hiking boots will help keep your feet steady on the trails and wet rocks. And don't forget your camera and plenty of film!

Despite the fact that the Victoria Falls area is drawing an increasing number of thrill-seekers looking to challenge the waters of the lower Zambezi, the most popular activity for tourists is still simply viewing the Falls them-selves—from across the chasm or high in the sky.

Niagara Falls (right) lies on the border between New York and Ontario, Canada, and is considered one of the most famous sights in North America. Visited by about 14 million people each year, Niagara Falls is much more accessible than Victoria Falls (opposite), but it is not nearly as spectacular in terms of height, width, or sheer presence.

Some of the best places from which to view the Falls are atop the steep cliff wall directly opposite the cataract, in Zimbabwe. Or hike the trails through the tropical forest down to the water's edge. Be sure to pack a rain jacket or umbrella, or you'll get soaked from the spray. To really feel the Falls' "thunder," hike to Danger Point, a rock slab jutting out into the river, at the foot of the Falls (the Zambia side has a similar feature called Knife Edge). From there, you can see the Boiling Pot, the place where the furiously churning waters of the Zambezi turn and head down

the zigzagging gorges. For a bird's eye view of the Falls, take the 15-minute "Flight of Angels" small aircraft or helicopter tour. For a panoramic view, linger on the Victoria Falls bridge.

Malaria-carrying mosquitoes love the damp conditions of the Falls area. You can reduce your chances of contracting the disease by taking preventative drugs; staying indoors between dusk and dawn, when mosquitoes are most active; using insect repellant; wearing loose, long-sleeved shirts and pants; and sleeping underneath a mosquito net at night.

VICTORIA  FALLS

QUICK FACTS

Location: On the border between Zimbabwe and Zambia, in southern Africa

Water source: The Zambezi River

Age: ~ Two million years

Falls width: Nearly one mile (1.6 km)

Falls height: About 350 feet (105 m), twice as high as Niagara Falls; spray can often be seen and "thunder" heard more than 20 miles (32 km) away

Average amount of water flow over the lip: More than 130 million gallons (490 million l) per minute

Season of heaviest water flow: March or April, the end of the rainy season

Climate: Subtropical, with an average temperature of 68 °F (20 °C)

First non-African to view the Falls: Scottish physician and missionary Dr. David Livingstone, in 1855, who named the Falls after Britain's Queen Victoria

National parks to which the Falls belong: Mosi-oa-Tunya National Park (Zambia), Victoria Falls National Park (Zimbabwe)

Vegetation: Tall hardwood trees such as ebony and mahagony; baobab, mopane, acacia, and sausage trees; figs and palms; a variety of ferns, mosses, grasses, and blooming herbs

Wildlife: Mammals such as elephants, zebras, antelope, hippos, monkeys, wildebeest, and giraffes; reptiles such as crocodiles, snakes, and various lizards; eagles, Taita falcons, hornbills, and other birds; hundreds of species of insects, including mosquitoes and flies

Other names: *Mosi-oa-Tunya,* an African name that translates to "Smoke That Thunders"

cataract—another word for "waterfall," especially a large one that falls over a steep ledge

commercialized—affected by the practice of buying and selling goods with an unhealthy emphasis on profit, often at the expense of people, animals, or the environment

conservationists—people who work for the protection of the earth's natural resources

contracted—got smaller; the opposite of expanded

erosive—related to the wearing away by wind, water, or chemicals; when soil erodes, its nutrients are carried away and plants cannot grow

escarpment—a steep slope or long cliff separating two relatively level surfaces

geologists—scientists who specialize in geology, the study of the earth's history and composition, including its crust (surface), interior, and types of rocks

gorges—narrow, steep-walled canyons often eroded by powerful, fast-moving water

indigenous—races or species that are native to, or have originated in, a particular region

lip—the top edge of a waterfall over which the water spills

malaria—a common, potentially fatal tropical disease characterized by fever and chills; it is spread by the bite of a parasite-carrying mosquito

missionary—a person sent by a religious group to convert others to a particular faith or to provide educational or medical help

rainforest—a tropical woodland that receives at least 100 inches (250 cm) of rain per year; its tall, broad-leaved trees form a continuous canopy overhead

safaris—hunting or sightseeing journeys or expeditions; typically associated with Africa

INDEX